Headlines 2

General editor John L. Foster

Survivors
From the Sea
Rod Hunt

Edward Arnold

© Roderick Hunt 1977

First published 1977 by
Edward Arnold (Publishers) Ltd
25 Hill Street, London W1X 8LL

ISBN 0 7131 0070 2

ACKNOWLEDGEMENTS
Drawings by Tony Morris.
The Publishers thank the following for permission to
reproduce copyright photographs: London Express News
and Feature Services (13, 35); Keystone Press (16);
J. Smailes and Son, Rhyl (33); Vickers Oceanics
Ltd. (37) Paul Elek Ltd and Kishiwa Yoshito (48).

Text set in 12/14 pt Monotype Baskerville, printed
by photolithography, and bound in Great Britain at
The Pitman Press, Bath

Contents

.

Alison's 20-hour Ordeal

The holiday began well. Alison Mitchell was looking forward to spending a week on board the motor yacht *Mariecelia*. Alison lived in Jersey in the Channel Islands and she was just 21. It would be fun to go across and see part of the French coast.

The boat belonged to Robert and Dolly Fraser. Alison had known them since she was a little girl. To her they were Uncle Bob and Auntie Dolly. Also going with them was their 25-year-old son Robert and his friend, Mike McCowen, aged 26.

Cold and Nasty

They left Jersey in bright sunshine and sailed to the French port of St Malo. The first part of the week was fine. Then the weather turned nasty. It became cold and wet. They decided to cut the holiday short and go home a day or two early.

Their last day was so cold that the stove in the galley was lit. That evening they went out for a meal to cheer themselves up. When they got back smoke was pouring from the front of the boat.

4

Because the stove was alight, a gas leak in the galley had started a fire. The galley was burned out. Now there was no heat or light.

The fire made them all want to get home as soon as they could. There had been strong winds. They would have to wait for the weather forecast next morning to see if they could leave.

A Rough Crossing

The next day was October 9th, 1964. Robert Fraser got up early to listen to the shipping forecast. He felt worried when he heard it. It would be a rough crossing to Jersey. Perhaps it would be better if the two women did not come. They could always make the crossing by plane. There was an airport quite near.

But Dolly and Alison said they would stay on board. It was only 40 miles to Jersey. All three men were used to boats. They knew they would be in good hands. If it was rough they could stay in their bunks. It would only be 4 or 5 hours before they were home.

The Worst Storm Ever

They did not know that the area would soon be hit by a terrible storm – the worst storm ever recorded. On Jersey tremendous winds had begun to batter the island. Roofs of houses were blown off. Trees were torn down. For some reason the *Mariecelia* had not heard the gale warning sent out at 10.15 a.m. While other ships headed for shelter, the *Mariecelia* headed on into the wind.

By mid morning, the *Mariecelia* was in the grip of the fierce gale. The boat rolled and pitched as it was pounded by giant waves. On board they could do nothing but hold on. Suddenly Dolly Fraser was flung across the deck-house floor. Her arm was broken. Alison did her best to make her aunt comfortable and to stop her being thrown about.

Huge Waves

Then a huge wave smashed through the forward deck-house window. The sea began to flood the saloon. Alison ran below and brought up two mattresses. They pushed them into the hole and for a while the sea was kept back.

They had been sailing for nearly 5 hours. They must be near land now. Mike McCowen put on a safety harness and went out on deck to look for the island. Between the great white-topped waves he just caught sight of the headland. The news made them all feel better. They began to talk of getting ashore for a good hot meal.

Washed Overboard

At that moment another huge wave broke over the
6

Mariecelia. It ripped off the deck-house as if it were
matchwood. Alison, who had been sitting there,
was sucked down inside the boat. She lost all
sense of time and place. Then the water dragged
her up and out in a returning gush.

　　She found herself clear of the boat and in the
sea. All round her was the broken wood from the
smashed boat. Alison blacked out and began to
go under. Then strong hands grabbed her. The
others were in the sea too. They had all been
washed from the boat. They clung together in the
crashing waves.

Alone in the Sea

Through the stormy sea the *Mariecelia* sailed on.
All her upper decking was gone, but her engines
were still running. The five friends watched in
horror as the boat sailed away without them. There
was nobody left on board and no hope of getting
back on the boat.

Jersey was only a few kilometres away. They
could just see the shoreline through the wind-
whipped sea. When the tide turned they might be
carried into shore. That would not be for 6 hours.
With no life-jackets, would they be able to keep
afloat for so long? In grim silence they clung to some
floating wood, and hoped.

So Near and Yet So Far

After some time they noticed that the shore
seemed closer. The tide was carrying them in.
Robert Fraser had made them kick their legs to
keep warm. Now they kicked to make themselves
move shorewards.

For a while they felt hopeful. Then the light
began to fade. Each one grew quiet. They began
to wonder if there was any hope left. When the
tide turned again, they would be carried back out
to sea. Now they had come so close to shore they
could see the houses. They even thought they could
make out people.

Drowned

As it grew dark, Dolly Fraser slipped away from the beam of wood they all clung to. Her broken arm had been painful. She no longer had the strength to hold on. She died so quickly and quietly that the others hardly knew she had gone.

Then Mike found himself in trouble. He had tied himself to the beam of wood while he dived under some wreckage to look for a flare gun. Now he could not untie the rope. The rope was getting shorter as the beam turned over and over in the water. Soon he would be dragged under.

Alison did her best to hold Mike up. Then she found his head was beneath the water. With horror she realised the rope had taken him down and he had drowned.

Grim Silence

The others clung on in grim silence. Then Jimmy Fraser told them he could no longer hold on. His face had been badly hurt in the wreck. He was finding it hard to breathe. Suddenly, he was no longer there. He, too, had died quietly, without fuss. Alison spoke carefully to Robert. She told him she was going to try to swim in to the shore. Robert agreed it was their best course, even though it meant letting go of the beam.

They swam together for a while. Then Robert began to slow. He told Alison to go ashore for help.

Alison told him to press on to a buoy a short way ahead. Robert did not answer. When Alison looked back he was gone. In half an hour she had lost all her friends. Now she was alone.

Carried Along the Coast

Looking towards the shore, she saw that the pattern of lights was changing. She knew she was being carried along the coast. Even though the tide had changed she felt she was not being swept backwards. A lighted buoy behind her showed her this.

In fact Alison was being carried eastwards round the southern tip of the island. There was a danger that she might be swept right out to sea.

But Alison did not give up. She kept on swimming and somehow the tides and currents took her up the east side of the island. For a long time she could see Castle Gorey. It jutted out into the sea, high on a cliff top. At night it was floodlit.

Desperate

She tried to swim towards the safety of Gorey Castle Harbour below the castle but she seemed to get no nearer. Suddenly the lights went out. It was midnight. They had all been switched off.

Now she began to feel desperate and very

alone. She did not stop swimming. As the hours
passed she lost all sense of direction. She felt she
was being taken away from land again. Slowly she
found herself giving up. All she wanted to do was
relax and let herself go. The sea could have her.

Fresh Hope

Somehow she pulled herself together. She must
not let go. She made herself think about her 21st
birthday party. She remembered the car her
father had given her as a present. In her mind she
planned a holiday in it once she was safe. She
began swimming again.

11

The cries of a seagull gave her fresh hope. She could not be far from land. She found she could not see out of her swollen eyes. It must now be light. Ahead of her she thought she could make out the shape of a low cloud on the water. She could swim towards that.

Ashore at Last

After what seemed like hours she heard the roar of pounding water. She was thrown about and the sea crashed round her. During the night the tide had taken her into the cliffs on the north side of the Island. The cloud she had seen was land. Now she was being pitched onto the rocky coast.

Somehow she pulled herself out of the water and collapsed. Above her rose cliffs 15 metres high. Forcing her eyes open, she saw a steep path. She began to drag herself upwards. The sharp wind froze her body. It was much colder than the sea. Her arms and legs were swollen and softened by the long hours in the water. Her skin was torn by the sharp rocks and boulders. She shivered violently. She willed herself to go on.

A Dreadful Sight

At the top of the cliff was a track which led to a narrow lane. A car was coming down the lane. Alison had help at last. But, as the car came close, she hid herself.

12

Her ordeal in the sea had swollen her arms and legs. They were white and horribly puffed up. Her head was cut and her hair matted with blood. She was wearing only her pants and a sweater. Alison needed help badly, but she could not bear to be seen. She dived into the bracken and hid. The car drove past and was gone.

Shortly afterwards she found herself in the yard of a nearby farm. She no longer cared what she must look like. To the farmer, Mr William de la Mare, she was a dreadful sight. Now she was safe, she could only jabber. Her head was so swollen that her eyes could not be seen. Her neck was twice its normal size. A pendant she was wearing had to be cut off. Her body was a mass of cuts and bruises.

It was 11.30 on the morning of October 10th. Alison had been in the water for 20 hours. She was taken to hospital and three weeks later had fully recovered from her ordeal.

Snatched To Safety

It had been a long hard trip for the men on the fishing boat *Jeanne Gougy*. For 10 days they had worked almost non-stop. Every two hours the great trawl nets had been pulled in heavy with fish. At last the holds were full. The captain and crew were pleased with the catch. They could sail home to France for a well-earned rest.

Then, as the ship left the fishing grounds south of Ireland, a terrible storm hit them. They had to battle against gale force winds and giant waves. Until the storm dropped there was no rest for the 18 men on board.

Dangerous Rocks

At last the wind dropped and the raging seas fell to a a heavy swell. By midnight the crew of the *Jeanne Gougy* could turn in. Three men were able to handle the boat and keep watch. The rest of the crew – 15 men – slept soundly below decks.

As the night wore on the fishing boat took sight of the Longships lighthouse, about 5 km off Land's End. Here there are dangerous rocks and reefs. In the wheel-house the three men steered a course to take the *Jeanne Gougy* safely to the west of the terrible Longships. The time was just after 04.00 hours.

Cape Cornwall is a high headland north of Land's End. Here there is a coastguard lookout hut. Since just before 04.30 hours the coastguard on duty had watched the dim red light of a ship. It passed to the east of the Longships lighthouse. It seemed to be going over far too close to the tip of Land's End.

The Wrong Course

The coastguard went outside with a signal lamp. He flashed the ship to warn it but there was no reply. What had happened to the helmsman and the men on watch? The coastguard could see the ship was sailing into danger.

The ship was the *Jeanne Gougy*. The time was now 05.10 hours. Somehow the men in the wheel-house had taken the wrong course. They had not seen the coastguard's signal and the ship had come right over towards the coast. Now she was steering herself straight on to the rocks of Land's End.

On the Rocks

Suddenly there was a terrible sound of tearing metal. With a grinding crash the ship rammed

15

onto the rocks. The men on watch were flung
forward against the wheel-house window. Below
deck, the sleeping men were thrown out of their
bunks. A giant hole was ripped in the ship's hull.

For a second everything seemed quiet. The
throbbing of the engines had stopped. The men,
still dazed with sleep, picked themselves up. Then
they heard a new sound, the gushing of water. It
flooded in through the jagged hole in the ship's
side. Huge waves broke over the ship and water
began to pour in from above. Within seconds the
men were up to their necks in sea water.

16

Out on Deck

Six of the men somehow got out on to the deck.
The cabins below had flooded at terrible speed.
They feared the rest of the men must have drowned
before they could get out.

One of the men, Michel Pade, spoke to the
others. He told them that their only chance was
to get across to the wheel-house. Already the ship
was tipping over. Great waves crashed over them.
If the ship went right over it would be too late.

Now or Never

The captain was among the six men. He looked
round at the others. One of them, the cabin boy,
Jean Ridel, was only 16 years old. It was only his
third trip on the *Jeanne Gougy*. The cook was there,
too, and the chief engineer. Michel Pade was right.
Somehow they must get over to the wheel-house.
It was now or never.

Between the smashing waves they scrambled
across the leaning deck. One by one they got to
the wheel-house and scrambled inside. No one
else was in the wheel-house. The three men on
watch had gone. They must have been swept away.

Inside the Wheel-house

The six men were in the same danger. The
ship was almost over on its side. The sea washed

17

right over it. At times it was right under the waves. The wheel-house was filled with water, but the men could still breathe as a pocket of air was trapped inside.

The captain looked at the others as they clung together. He knew it would be a miracle if any of them were saved, even if rescue came.

In fact rescue teams were already close to the wreck. Two lifeboats had been called by the Cape Cornwall coastguard on his radio. These boats were close by but they could not get very near the broken ship in such heavy seas.

Rescue Teams

On the cliff-top, high above the wreck, the coastguard Rescue Team was in action. Special searchlights were set up to light the wreck below. Rope-firing guns were ready to fire a line to anyone still alive.

The Rescue Team had seen the men make their way to the wheel-house. A flare was sent into the air which lit up the whole scene. Then the first line was fired. It landed near the wheel-house but no one grabbed it. A second line was fired. This time an arm reached out from the wheel-house. It could not reach the line.

Terrible Failure

A third line was fired. Now the wheel-house door

was pushed open. One of the trapped men crawled out and grabbed it. It looked as if the men might now be saved by using the line. But then a huge wave broke over the ship. As it fell away, the rescue team saw with horror that the man had gone with it. The door of the wheel-house has been torn off too.

The force of the wave was met by another surge of water. It curled over the broken wheel-house and sucked down inside. The coastguards saw the other men being swept out as if they were corks from a bottle. In seconds they had gone from sight and the wheel-house was silent and still. The rescuers felt bitter. Their rescue attempt had ended in terrible failure.

By now the ship was fully under water. It could only be seen when the waves rolled away from it. Surely nobody could still be alive on board.

Rescue Helicopter

As daylight came an R.A.F. rescue helicopter got to the wreck. It flew low over the ship and the coast around it. All they could see was floating wreckage from the *Jeanne Gougy*. Then they saw the body of a man in the water. He was picked up by the helicopter and rushed to hospital, but it was too late to save him.

The lifeboats found two more bodies in the sea. It seemed the unlucky crew of the *Jeanne*

19

Gougy had all been drowned. Even so, none of the rescue teams gave up. If there was even a small chance of a man being found alive, they would be there to save him.

On the cliff the Coastguard Rescue Team stared at the wreck. The ship had been under water for 6 hours. Now they could begin to see the wheel-house again. As soon as the tide was low enough they would try to go on board.

A Face at a Window

As they stared at the wheel-house they could hardly believe their eyes. There was a face at one of the upturned windows. Someone was alive down there after all. A line was fired and the man's hand reached out and pulled the line in.

It was Michel Pade. Somehow he had clung on when the sea had gushed down into the wheel-house. He had seen the others being swept out. Using all his strength he had hung on. There had been just enough air trapped round him to keep him alive.

Now at last rescue was near. But Pade was too weak to get into the harness the Rescue Team had sent down the line. It was all he could do to fix the line to the wheel-house. Someone would have to help him. The only hope was to use the helicopter, which was back at base getting more fuel.

20

Special Harness

Then there was a shout from the rescuers. Four men had climbed out of a porthole. They were standing on the ship's rail. How had they kept alive under water for so long?

The men had been trapped in their cabins as soon as the ship filled with water. Somehow they had clung together in an air lock. Only their heads had been above water. A porthole in the ship's starboard side was above them. They could not get through it because the sea had been washing over it.

Now their ordeal was nearly over. A line was fired from the cliff top by the Rescue Team. The men were able to fix it to the rail. Then one by one they were taken off the ship in a special harness.

A Dangerous Job

By now the helicopter was on the scene. Winchman Eric Smith would have to go down and strap Michel Pade to the winch cable. It would be a dangerous job. Pade was inside the wheel-house. Smith would have to go in too. In such strong winds, his own cable might catch on the spars or rigging on the boat. Then the two men would be trapped below.

To make matters worse, great gusts of spray were being blown over the ship. The helicopter crew would find it hard to see Eric Smith through the spray. The gusts of wind from the cliff top made it hard to keep the helicopter at an even height.

Still Alive

Eric Smith could not help feeling afraid. The wind and spray whipped him as he went down. All

round him were ropes, nets, masts and spars. He reached the ship's rail and grabbed it as a huge wave broke over him. Another wave swamped him as he carefully made his way into the wheel-house.

At first he could not see Michel Pade. Then he saw a passage-way, leading from the wheel-house. Eric Smith stared in surprise. Behind the limp figure was another man lying quite still. It was the 16-year-old cabin boy Jean Ridel. Eric Smith saw that the boy was still alive. He would have to get Michel Pade up to the helicopter, then come back for Jean Ridel.

Courage and Skill

It took all Eric Smith's courage and skill to get the first man up on the cable winch, then go back for the second. As the helicopter fought to keep steady against the wind, Smith took each limp body through the mass of wires and masts to safety.

Then, in case any more men were alive on board, he went back down. Again and again he shouted into the passage-way but there was no answer. To make sure, Smith went down yet again. He looked through every porthole and hatchway above the water. But there was no sign of life.

Only six men had come out alive from the wreck. Without the courage of the rescuers they would all have died.

The Boys Who Were Blown Out to Sea

David and John Mullins were excited. It was the start of their holiday at the seaside. The Mullins family had rented a bungalow on the Welsh coast. The bungalow was beside some sand dunes. The sea was right behind them.

David was 10 and John was 6. With their mum and dad and baby sister, Pat, they were looking forward to a week playing on the sandy beach. It would be really good this year. David had got his dad to bring the rubber dinghy.

Dangerous

John Mullins, their father, had brought the dinghy home to make a paddling pool in the garden. It was a big R.A.F. rescue dinghy. It could easily hold six men. John Mullins told the boys how dangerous dinghies could be. They could be swept out to sea by winds or tides.

At first Mr Mullins did not want to take the dinghy with them. John and David said they did not want to take the rubber boat out far. They could fix it to a rope. That way it would be quite safe. In the end Mr Mullins gave in. The dinghy was packed with their things.

24

Lifeline

They waited for a calm sunny day. Wednesday
began well. At last they could take the dinghy out.
That morning the boys helped their father blow it
up. It took a long time. It was the afternoon
before they took it down to the beach.

A lifeline 100 metres long was fixed to the
dinghy. Mr Mullins dug a hole and anchored the
line in the sand. Then the family waded to the
dinghy to try it out. They were still dressed, as
they had only taken off their shoes and socks.

It was such good fun that they did not see the
sky was getting dark. A wind began to get up.
Then a wave broke over the boat and splashed
them. Mrs Mullins climbed out and waded ashore
carrying baby Pat.

Blown Out to Sea

Suddenly Mr Mullins looked at the shore. It
seemed to be quite far off. Then he knew why.
The line had pulled away from its anchor in the
sand. The boat was being blown out to sea.

Out of his Depth

At once Mr Mullins jumped out of the dinghy. He
intended to wade ashore pulling the boat behind
him. But once in the water he found it too deep for
him to stand up.

In this part of Wales the coast is very sandy. But the sand is not smooth and flat. It rises and falls in gullies, so that the water is deep in some places and shallow in others.

Mr Mullins had got out of the dinghy in a deep gully. He was right out of his depth. He must swim ashore and pull the boat behind him. But he was not a strong swimmer. Soon he was tired and he knew he was not getting very far. To make matters worse the boys began to feel afraid. They stood up in the boat. Mr Mullins had to shout at them to sit down.

Some swimmers were in the sea a little way off. Mr Mullins called to them to swim out and help him. But the swimmers were afraid of the strong currents and wind. They did not feel able to swim out to the dinghy.

In Difficulty

Mr Mullins felt the only hope was to go and get help himself. He told the boys to sit still. Then he let go of the dinghy and struck out for the shore. Not being a good swimmer he was soon in trouble. He had to fight his way against the strong drift of the wind and sea.

Back on the beach Mrs Mullins saw her husband in difficulty. There were only a few people on the beach. None of them seemed able to help. She ran up to a strange woman and thrust her baby at her. 'Look after her for me,' she gasped and then she ran down the beach and into the sea.

Dorothy Mullins was also a poor swimmer, but somehow she reached her husband. His strength was nearly gone, but he was still only halfway across the deep gully. Together they struggled in the water. Then three men walking down the beach saw them. They rushed into the water and somehow got them ashore.

Emergency

Mr and Mrs Mullins lay on the sand sick with shock and with the sea water they had swallowed. Far out, the dinghy could only be seen when it bobbed up in the choppy waves. Mrs Mullins struggled to her feet and tried to run back into the water. She felt she must try to swim out to reach

27

her sons. One of the men stopped her. Another had already raced off to phone for help. Mr Mullins was too tired and weak to move. He sat with his head in his hands.

The 999 emergency call was put through to the coastguard at Rhyl just after 4 o'clock. Soon the loud bang of maroons was heard, calling the lifeboat crew. 'A rubber dinghy with two boys in it drifting out to see off the Point of Air Lighthouse.' Within minutes the lifeboat was launched.

Further and Further Out to Sea

Meanwhile, in the dinghy, John and David Mullins obeyed their father's last shout telling them to keep still. They lay flat in the bottom of the boat, feeling only its rise and fall as it rode the waves. Once or twice they looked over the edge. The figures on the shore were getting smaller. They thought they could see their mother waving at them. When they looked again they could not make out the figures any more. Then even the beach was out of sight.

John began to feel afraid. David tried to comfort him. He told him not to worry. They would soon drift on to an island. They would find a house to phone from. Then their dad would come and pick them up. But all he could see was the empty sea.

He tried to grab a floating buoy but it was out of reach. He was just able to throw the lifeline over it. For a second or two the rope went tight as the buoy held it. Then the drag of the dinghy pulled it loose again. David could still see the lighthouse. They seemed to be drifting to the north-east of it.

An 'Island'

Suddenly David found he could see the bottom of the sea. The dinghy seemed to be in shallow water. Could they be coming to an island? Then the boys saw a sweep of sand ahead. It was a sandy island. They felt it would be best to land on the island. The firm sand felt more secure than the frail rubber and canvas dinghy. They dragged it high up away from the water and buried the line in the sand.

They could see no sign of life anywhere. There was no house for them to phone from. There was nothing to see but sand. All they could do was to wait for someone to come and find them.

Then great curtains of rain began to slant down. They could see nothing at all now. Gusts of sand-filled wind ripped over them, stinging their legs. The rain drove into them. David told John to help him turn the dinghy over. They could shelter underneath it. Perhaps when the rain stopped they could set out and find someone.

Goodbye to the Dinghy

As they tried to turn the dinghy, the strong winds caught it. It was torn from their grasp. The force of the gust lifted it up in the air to carry it away. The boys watched in horror as the dinghy bounced across the sand. It turned over and over as it went. It was impossible to catch it before it reached the water. Helplessly David and John watched their only means of safety floating away from them. In seconds, the wind had blown the dinghy far out to sea. Then it vanished.

Trapped in the Sea

The boys were stunned. Then David saw something else that made his heart jump with fear. The 'island' was getting smaller. When they had first landed, the sand stretched away out of sight. Now he could see water on all sides. They were not on an island at all but on a sandbank in the sea. If the tide was coming in, it would cover the sand. As it rose, it would cover them too!

John, too, had begun to see the water creeping nearer. David tried to sound cheerful. 'They're bound to send a boat soon,' he said.

Nowhere to Go

On the sandbank the water slid over the last small patch of sand. David and John stood together. Now they had nowhere to go. Soon the water was above their feet, then their ankles. They felt sick with fear as the cold water crept upwards.

Before long the sea was above John's waist, then his armpits. In the end David lifted him up on his back. It was hard for him to hold his brother up. His feet kept sinking in the sand so he could not stand firmly.

As the water reached the top of his arms, David knew he would soon have to let John go. It would not be long now before the water was washing over their heads.

31

There's Something There!

All this time the lifeboat had been heading out
towards them. Rescue work is difficult along this
part of the coast. The seabed is uneven and there
are many sandbanks. Lifeboats can easily run
aground.

As they neared where they thought the boys
must be, the crewmen kept a sharp lookout.
Suddenly one of them spotted something. 'There's
something there!' The men in the lifeboat strained
their eyes. 'Like two footballs. It could be boys'
heads.'

32

Stuck Fast

Soon they could see the boys clearly. There was
no time to lose or the sea would cover them. Then
the lifeboat grounded and stuck fast. It would
float free as the tide rose, but by then it would be
too late.

Two crewmen jumped over the side to wade
to the boys. They got to them just as the water
was washing over David's face. He was still
holding John just clear of the water.

A large crowd greeted the lifeboat as it got
back to the boathouse. Mr and Mrs Mullins heard
the news that both boys were safe. Only later,
when they heard the full story, did they learn
what a remarkable escape they had had.

Shipwrecked Under the Sea

The two men inside the mini-submarine were thrown backwards. 'My God, we're sinking!' One minute the mini sub was on the surface, the next it was going down like a sinking bottle. The sea bed was 520 metres below. What would happen when the mini sub hit the bottom? Roger Mallinson stared at the control panel. The dials spun as they plunged downwards. What had happened to make the mini-sub sink?

The mini sub was called *Pisces III*. The tiny craft was one of only a few such submarines. They were fitted with remote control 'hands'. These were worked from inside the sub. *Pisces III* had been laying telephone cables along the bottom of the Atlantic Ocean. The cable had to be buried in the sand and mud of the seabed. It was a difficult and dangerous job for the sub's two-man crew.

Roger Chapman and Roger Mallinson had been down on the seabed all that day. They were tired but the work had gone well. They had put down a kilometre of cable. They were ready to return to the surface. They telephoned their mother ship *Voyager* to say 'We're coming up.'

Twisted Towline

It took 30 minutes for the sub to reach the surface.
Then a diver in a rubber motor-boat brought a
tow-line to the mini sub. The line was fixed on
so that *Pisces* could be winched on to *Voyager*.

Suddenly the diver waved and shouted.
Somehow the tow-line had twisted round the
catch on the rear air chamber door. The diver was
too late to stop the line pulling tight. The catch
opened and the door pulled off. Over a ton of
water rushed into the chamber. *Pisces* began to
sink!

35

Stuck on the Seabed

Inside the sub, Mallinson and Chapman did what
they could to protect themselves when the sub
hit bottom. They turned off the power to stop
fire, and put all their things away. They padded
their legs and bit on rags to stop themselves biting
their tongues.

Then the mini sub hit the seabed. The crash
was not as bad as they feared. It had hit the
bottom tail down and sunk in two or three feet
of mud. The two men checked the damage. No
water was anywhere in the hold. The power was
still working. The air supply was all right. They
had light to see by and air to breathe. They were
still able to contact *Voyager* by phone. But how
long would it be before rescue came?

No diver could survive so deep below the
surface. The only way to rescue *Pisces* was to use
another mini sub. The sub's metal 'hands' could
fix strong cables to the sunken craft. *Pisces* could
then be winched slowly to the surface.

A Long Wait

There were only two other mini submarines
operating at that time. Both were a long way
away. One was laying pipes in Canada. The other
was in the North Sea. The subs would have to be
flown to the nearest port and *Voyager* would have
to speed there to pick them up.

This might take a long time. *Voyager* could not leave the sunken *Pisces* until another ship took her place. It was important to keep contact with the two trapped men. It would be some time before the rescue could even begin.

The inside of the mini sub *Pisces* is not much bigger than a family car. Chapman and Mallinson sat close together to keep warm. The sub had tipped back almost upright in the mud. It was cold and very damp. The men ate what little food they had. They waited and waited.

The Deepest Rescue Ever

It was 9 hours before another ship replaced *Voyager*. The race was now on. The mini sub had an air supply to last three days. Already nearly a day's

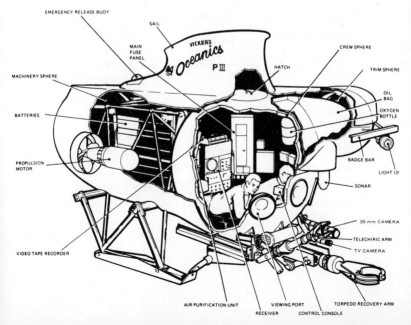

supply had been used. It would take *Voyager* at least a day to come back with the two rescue submarines. That left only one day to bring the sub up. The mini sub was very deep. At 520 metres, this would be the deepest rescue ever tried in sea history. Something could easily go wrong!

Early on the morning of the third day, *Voyager* was back. The two mini subs were on board. They had been waiting at the port. At once they prepared to begin the rescue. A special hook was made. It was like an anchor which opened and shut like an umbrella. The hook was to be put inside the open hatch of the flooded air chamber. When the arms were opened, the hook would hold firm. Then *Pisces* could be pulled up.

Out of Action

One of the mini subs, *P2*, was sent down to fix the hook. The hook was on a special floating cable. *P2* was only a few feet away from *Pisces* when the hook suddenly broke free. *P2's* remote control arm bent, putting it out of action. The pull on the floating cable had been too strong.

On the radio telephone Chapman and Mallinson heard the news that *P2* had not been able to fix the hook. They were told not to worry. The second sub *P5* was on its way with a new kind of hook. The trapped men were not told that there were gale force winds on the surface. The strong winds and rough seas were making the rescue even more difficult.

Another Failure

P5 was no luckier than *P2*. At first she could not even find *Pisces*. Something had gone wrong with her electric homing gear. This was put right but it had taken *P5* $5\frac{1}{2}$ hours to reach the trapped sub. Then, just as *P5* placed the hook on *Pisces* it slipped off. *P5* grabbed it but could not get the hook in the right place. In the end the hook was fixed to a part of the sub that was not strong. It could not be used to lift *Pisces* from the seabed. Now the second rescue bid had failed.

On the surface, no one had slept for 60 hours. The men worked with frantic haste to repair *P2*. Nearly a quarter of a mile below the surface Mallinson and Chapman began to feel the effects of their long hours in the cold, cramped submarine.

Running Out of Time

It was now the mid-evening of the third day. At last *P2* was ready to dive. But by now the seas were so rough that it was dangerous to launch her. When she was put into the waves her water alarm rang out. She had to be pulled in to check for leaks. More time was wasted – and time was running out. At last *P2* was cleared and once more sent

39

down with the umbrella hook. This time she was lucky. It took only an hour to fix the hook in place.

It was 72 hours since *Pisces* had sunk. The air supply was due to run out in two or three hours. No one was sure that the line now fixed on by *P2* would be strong enough. To make sure, a second line must be fixed to the sub.

CURV to the Rescue

Luckily another rescue craft had been sent from America. This was an un-manned submarine called *CURV*. It was worked from the surface by remote control. *CURV* had the right gear to fix a second line on to *Pisces*. It had arrived just in time. *CURV* was sent down to *Pisces* and in only an hour had put a second line on her.

At last the trapped sub could be brought to the surface. Slowly the lifting gear began to turn. In a swirl of mud, *Pisces* began to lift off from the seabed. The rough sea above made the mother ship rise and fall. The mini sub on the cables bobbed up and down as well. The cables took a terrible strain. The hooks jerked up and down. Everyone held their breath. At 20 metres from the surface a diver was sent down to fix a heavy cable to *Pisces*. At last she was safe.

Mallinson and Chapman had been trapped for three days and four hours. The rescuers had made it only just in time.

37 days Adrift in an Open Boat

At 10 a.m. on June 15th, 1972, killer whales
attacked a small schooner in the middle of the
Pacific Ocean. 60 seconds later the boat had sunk.

There was only time to cut free the tiny dinghy
lashed to the deck and to launch the boat's rubber
life raft. Those 60 seconds were terrible for the
six on board the schooner. They grabbed a few
things and scrambled into the life raft. Then it was
all over. The schooner was gone. They were alone
on the vast and empty sea in a small rubber raft.
Fixed to the raft was the tiny dinghy.

Stunned

Two of them began to cry. They were twins called
Neil and Sandy and they were only 11 years old.
Their father put his arm round Neil and looked
at his wife. She too had tears in her eyes. Douglas
their 17-year-old son looked stunned. So did Robin,
a 22-year-old student who was travelling with
them.

Dougal Robertson, the father, had been a
farmer. Just over 18 months before, he had sold

his farm to buy the boat. He and his wife had used all their money making the boat into a home for the family. They wanted to educate their children by taking them round the world. Now the boat was gone, they had lost everything.

Little Chance

In the tiny life raft, Mr Robertson began to think out what they must do to be saved. He knew they had little chance of being rescued. Nobody would miss them for at least five weeks. Even then, no one would know where to start searching for them in 4800 km of ocean. They could not expect to see a passing ship. Shipping did not cross this part of the Pacific.

Mrs Robertson put her husband's thoughts into words. 'We must get these boys to land,' she said.

Slowly and carefully Mr Robertson spoke to his family. They must try to sail about 600 km north. They would then be in a shipping lane. Someone might spot them. If not, they must find the current to take them to the coast of central America, 1100 km further on.

Short Supplies

They made a check of all they had. In the survival kit was special bread and glucose, but only enough for a few days. There was also fishing gear, a knife, flares and a signal mirror, a torch and a first aid kit. They only had 18 pints of fresh water. If there was no rain they would soon suffer from lack of drinking water.

They had also saved from the wreck some biscuits, a few onions, 10 oranges and 6 lemons, some sweets and half a pound of glucose. They found Mrs Robertson's sewing basket floating in the sea. It was full of useful bits and pieces. Another lucky find was a large canvas sail with a wire edge.

Cramped, Cold and Frightened

As they settled down for the night in the tiny raft, Mrs Robertson said a prayer and sang a hymn. Then, while one of them kept watch, they tried to sleep. Darkness fell and it grew cold. The life-raft rose and fell in the waves. Large fish called dorados bumped them from underneath. Frightened and uncomfortable they spent the first of 37 nights on the open sea.

As the days passed, the Robertsons and Robin, their passenger, tried to get used to living in the rubber raft. They were sailing about 32 km a day, but the raft was losing air all the time. Every 15 minutes it had to be blown up to keep it hard and firm. This was a tiring job for Douglas, Robin or Mr Robertson to keep up.

Lack of Water

Sometimes flying fish landed on the raft. They ate
these with pieces of lemon or onion. The main
worry was lack of water. They tried to make do on
less then half a pint a day each. Mr Robertson
knew there would be plenty of rain once they got
to an area of the ocean called the Doldrums. This
was 600 km away. Some rain did fall. They caught
it as it ran from the roof of the raft. It was yellow
and tasted salty and rubbery.

On the sixth day they caught a 16-kg
dorado fish. They cut it up and ate until they were
full. They found the spine of the fish good to chew.
It was full of fresh water. Robin chewed the head.
Later they found it was good to suck the eyes of the
fish. The eyes have vitamins and were very good
for them.

Terrible Thirst

Already they were much thinner. The salt water
began to rot their clothes. Their skin was raw
where they had been sitting for so long. The heat
during the day gave them a terrible thirst. They
chewed rubber to try to stop their mouths going
dry. They took little sips of water from time to
time.

Then they saw a ship. It was passing about
three miles away. With shaking hands,

Mr Robertson lit a signal rocket. It shot high into the air. The ship did not seem to change course. Another rocket was sent off in a bright streak of light. The ship was already getting smaller. Finally it was gone from sight. It had not seen the distress signal.

Survive!

At first Mr Robertson felt angry and bitter. Then he told himself that it was no good hoping for rescue. The only hope was to survive. He looked at the twins. His wife had been right. They must get them to land. They would fight the sea and they would survive.

They had good luck that day. They caught an 36-kg turtle. It was good to eat and it was full of eggs. Turtles gave them a good supply of meat after that.

Mrs Robertson began to see to the salt water boils on their skin. It would be hard to keep them fit and healthy. As a nurse she knew they must keep clean and do exercises. She was still worried about lack of drinking water.

Into the Dinghy

On the 15th day the dinghy broke free. Mr Robertson heard Douglas yell. The dinghy was 60 metres away, trailing its tow wire. He knew they could not survive without it. At once he dived into the sea and raced towards it.

His family watched him helplessly. They could see a shark close behind him. He got to the dinghy just in time. It was a long time before he had the strength to bring the dinghy back. If they had lost it they would have lost their lives.

Two days later the rubber raft sank. It had been leaking air faster and faster. At last they could not keep it blown up at all. They moved into the tiny dinghy. It was too small for them to lie down properly and it was low in the water. They had come 600 km in 17 days. They still had another 1100 km to go.

46

Food

The days passed in the cramped and uncomfortable dinghy. Often they would pass the time by playing word games or telling stories. Neil and Sandy loved to talk about food. They would all play a game where one would tell the other about a favourite meal – ice cream, steak, stews, bacon and eggs – they talked on and on. In fact all they had in the boat were strips of dried turtle meat.

They were glad whenever they caught a turtle. Often they were full of creamy rich eggs. They found the oil from the turtles very good for them. Mrs Robertson rubbed it on their sore skin and boils. She found a way for the twins to eat the oil so that it did not make them sick. She knew it would help to keep them well.

Sharks

By the 32nd day they were down to only 5 pints of water. There had been no rain for some time. Mr Robertson caught three large dorado. They could chew these to get a little water. Even so, in the heat of the day they lay panting for a drink. They only took sips of their precious supply.

Sharks were never far away. There was always the fear that they might attack the boat and upset it. On the 37th night a shark did ram the dinghy. It was much longer than the boat and it attacked twice. Mr Robertson beat it off with a paddle.

The Ship

The next day began like any other. Then some
rain fell and they caught several fish. They were
filled with hope that they would last out. They
were busy sorting supplies of fish and turtle meat
when they saw a ship. They could hardly believe it.

Quickly they pulled out the flares and lit one.
Mr Robertson stood on the edge of the dinghy
and held the flare as high as he could. He could
see the ship clearly. It was a Japanese fishing boat.
He threw the flare up as high as he could and
tried to light another one. Then he saw the ship
had changed course. She was sailing towards
them. Rescue had come at last.